Down to Earth
Children's Leader Guide

Down to Earth:
The Hopes & Fears of All the Years Are Met in Thee Tonight

Down to Earth
978-1-5018-2339-8
978-1-5018-2340-4 eBook
978-1-5018-2341-1 Large Print

Down to Earth: Leader Guide
978-1-5018-2342-8
978-1-5018-2343-5 eBook

Down to Earth: Devotions for the Season
978-1-5018-2344-2
978-1-5018-2345-9 eBook

Down to Earth: Youth Study Book
978-1-5018-2352-7
978-1-5018-2353-4 eBook

Down to Earth: DVD
978-1-5018-2346-6

Down to Earth: Children's Leader Guide
978-1-5018-2354-1

Also by Mike Slaughter

Change the World

Christmas Is Not Your Birthday

Dare to Dream

Hijacked

Momentum for Life

Money Matters

Real Followers

Renegade Gospel

shiny gods

Spiritual Entrepreneurs

The Christian Wallet

The Passionate Church

UnLearning Church

Upside Living in a Downside Economy

For more information, visit www.MikeSlaughter.com.

Children's Leader Guide
by Susan Groseclose

Abingdon Press / Nashville

**Down to Earth
The Hopes & Fears of All the Years
Are Met in Thee Tonight**

Children's Leader Guide
by Susan Groseclose

*Copyright © 2016 Abingdon Press
All rights reserved.*

No part of this work may be reproduced or transmitted in any form or by any means, electronic or mechanical, including photocopying and recording, or by any information storage or retrieval system, except as may be expressly permitted by the 1976 Copyright Act or in writing from the publisher. Requests for permission can be addressed to Permissions, The United Methodist Publishing House, PO Box 280988, 2222 Rosa L. Parks Blvd., Nashville, TN 37228-0988 or e-mailed to permissions@umpublishing.org.

Local churches which have purchased this book may photocopy the pages within the book specifically labeled as "reproducible" for use with the lessons as indicated, provided each copy retains the copyright notice printed thereon: **Copyright © 2016 Abingdon Press** · *Permission is granted to photocopy this page for local church use only.*

This book is printed on elemental chlorine-free paper.
ISBN 978-1-5018-2354-1

Scripture quotations are from the Common English Bible. Copyright © 2011 by the Common English Bible. All rights reserved. Used by permission. www.CommonEnglishBible.com.

16 17 18 19 20 21 22 23 24 25 — 10 9 8 7 6 5 4 3 2 1
MANUFACTURED IN THE UNITED STATES OF AMERICA

Contents

To the Leader 7

1. Love 10

2. Be Humble 24

3. Serve 38

4. Be Grateful 52

To the Leader

This Children's Leader Guide is designed for use with Mike Slaughter and Rachel Billups's book and program, *Down to Earth*. This guide includes four lessons that prepare children to celebrate Jesus' birth. They will learn how Jesus came down to earth to show us a new way to live. Jesus came down to earth to show us how to love others, how to be humble, how to serve others, and how to express our gratitude.

The lessons in this guide, designed for children in grades K-2 and 3-6, are presented in a large-group/small-group format. Children begin with time spent at activity centers, followed by time together as a large group. Children end the lesson in small groups determined by grade. Each lesson plan contains the following sections:

Focus for the Teacher

The information in this section will provide you with background information about the week's lesson. Use this section for your own study as you prepare.

Explore Interest Groups

In this section, you'll find ideas for a variety of activity centers. The activities will prepare the children to hear the day's Scripture. Allow the children to choose one or more of the activities that interest them.

Large Group

Following the activity centers, the children will come together as a large group. This section begins with a transition activity followed by the story or a Bible verse activity. A worship time with lighting of the Advent Wreath concludes the large group time.

Small Groups

Children are divided into grade-level groups for small group time. Depending on the size of your class, you may need to have more than one group of younger or older children. It is recommended that each small group contain no more than ten children.

Young Children
The activities in this section are designed for children in grades K-2.

Older Children
The activities in this section are designed for children in grades 3-6.

Reproducible Pages

At the end of each lesson are reproducible pages, to be photocopied and handed out for the children to use during that lesson's activities.

Schedule

Many churches have weeknight programs that include an evening meal, an intergenerational gathering time, and classes for children, youth, and adults. The following schedule illustrates one way to organize a weeknight program.

5:30	Meal
6:00	Intergenerational gathering introducing weekly themes and places for the lesson. This time may include presentations, skits, music, and opening or closing prayers.
6:15–7:15	Classes for children, youth, and adults.

Churches may want to do this study as a Sunday school program. This setting would be similar to the weeknight setting. The following schedule takes into account a shorter class time which is the norm for Sunday morning programs.

10 minutes	Intergenerational gathering
45 minutes	Classes for children, youth, and adults

Choose a schedule that works best for your congregation and its Christian education programs.

Blessings to you and the children as you learn and experience why Jesus came down to earth!

Down to Earth
Children's Leader Guide

1 Love

Objectives
The children will:
- Explore how Advent prepares us for Jesus to come down to earth.
- Experience a Bible story to learn how Jesus teaches us to love one another.
- Practice our down-to-earth mission to love others.

Theme
Jesus came down to earth to show us how to love others.

Bible Verse
"Complete my joy by thinking the same way, having the same love, being united, and agreeing with each other." (Philippians 2:2)

Focus for the Teacher

Welcome to *Down to Earth*! Advent, the first season in the Christian year, is a time to prepare for the birth of Jesus. These four weeks of Advent, we will be exploring our belief that Jesus came down to earth to teach us how to live. Learning activities based on the weekly Bible verse and key theme will provide opportunities for children to discover and experience living like Jesus.

Each week, we will light an Advent wreath as we wait and anticipate Jesus' birth. Children will also make a Christmas ornament to remind them of the week's key word. These ornaments can be hung on a tree in the classroom and used to review the weekly lessons. The session will end with a small group activity for the children to practice living out Jesus' down-to-earth teaching.

This week, children will learn that Jesus came down to earth to show us how to love others. Paul wrote to the Philippians that we are to love like Jesus. The good Samaritan is a familiar Bible story that illustrates Jesus' down-to-earth love.

> Like Jesus, we show God's love to others.

Children can live like Jesus by showing love to others. Older children have often experienced what it feels like to be hurt by another person's actions or words. They can relate to the people in the good Samaritan story who do not show love as well as the Samaritan. We will practice our down-to-earth mission to love others.

As you help children understand how to love like Jesus, think about your own life. When is it easy to show love? When do you find it difficult? Where have you seen children in your class showing love? What has recently happened in your church or community that illustrates Jesus' down-to-earth love?

Down to Earth: Children's Leader Guide

Explore Interest Groups

Be sure that adult leaders are waiting when the first child arrives. Greet and welcome the children. Get the children involved in an activity that interests them and introduces the theme for the day's activities.

They'll Know We Are Christians by Our Love

- **Say**: Jesus came down to earth to show us how to love. Other people will know that we are Christians, that we are followers of Jesus when we show love to others.

- Encourage the children to sing, "They'll Know We Are Christians."

- **Ask**: What are some ways that we show our love to God and others? (pray, using kind words, care for others, smile, send get-well card, forgive, and so forth)

- Sing the phrase, "They'll know we are Christians by our love" several times, and instead of saying "by our love," insert ways that children have identified. For example: "when we care," "when we forgive," or "by our actions."

Prepare

✓ Check a hymnal or YouTube for a version of the song "They'll Know We Are Christians."

Advent Wreath

- **Say**: Advent is the time when we get ready for Jesus' birth, when Jesus came down to earth. Today, we are going to work together to make an Advent wreath.

- Lay the Styrofoam wreath flat on a table.

- Give one candle each to four children and ask them to stand around the wreath. Have the children insert the four candles on top of the wreath at the 12:00, 3:00, 6:00, and 9:00 position as a clock.

- Have the rest of the children add evergreen to the wreath until the Styrofoam is covered.

- **Say**: We will use this Advent wreath each week in our worship time.

Prepare

✓ Provide one green Styrofoam wreath, artificial or live greenery, cutting shears, florist tape, and four blue or purple taper candles. (If you prefer not to light candles in the classroom, twist a piece of yellow tissue paper and attach to the candles to represent flame.)

✓ Before class, use scissors or a small knife to cut holes in the Styrofoam for the four candles at the 12:00, 3:00, 6:00, and 9:00 positions as a clock.

Love

Prepare

✓ Print out enough copies of **Reproducible 1a: Same or Different?**, found at the end of the lesson, so there is one for each child.

✓ Provide pencils.

Same or Different?

- Give each child a copy of **Same or Different?**

- **Say**: In this activity, you will find out what you have that's the same or different from another person in the class.

- Pair children. It will be helpful to pair an older child with a younger child.

- **Say**: Read each statement and decide whether your answer is the same or different. Put a check under the correct heading.

- Wait until children have finished their sheets.

- **Ask**: What are some ways you are the same? What are some ways you are different? I wonder what we have that's the same as Jesus.

- **Say**: These next few weeks, we are going to discover what we have that's the same as Jesus. We will explore how we are to think and act like Jesus. Today, we will learn how to love like Jesus.

Prepare

✓ Cut a 3-inch diameter circle out of white cardstock for each child.

✓ Provide a hole punch, red or green yarn, a red ink pad, and baby wipes or rubbing alcohol to remove the ink.

Thumbprint Heart Ornament

- **Say**: These next four weeks, we will be making Christmas ornaments to help us remember why Jesus was born. Today we are making a thumbprint heart ornament to remind us that Jesus came down to earth to show us how to love others.

- Give each child a circle.

- Help each child press their thumb on the ink pad then at an angle on the circle and repeat in the opposite direction, creating a heart shape. Help the children clean their thumbs using baby wipes or rubbing alcohol.

- At the top of each ornament, punch a hole for the yarn hanger.

- Cut a piece of yarn and thread it through the hole. Tie and knot the end.

- **Ask**: What does the thumbprint ornament remind us?

- **Say**: We remember that Jesus came down to show us how to love others. We will hang up our ornaments in class each week. At the end of the session, you can take your ornaments home to add to your tree.

Love Is...

- **Ask**: What does it mean to love others?
- **Say**: Today we are going to learn how to love like Jesus.
- Give each child a copy of **Love Is...**
- **Say**: Look up in your Bible, Matthew 25:25-26. Read the verse and fill in the blanks to discover how Jesus tells us to love others. Encourage the older children to help the younger children. (Bible quotations use the Common English Bible translation, but children should be able to fill in blanks using other translations also.)
- Wait until the children have finished their sheets.
- **Ask**: What are some other ways that we can love like Jesus?
- **Say**: Today we are going to hear a Bible verse that shows how we are to love like Jesus.

Prepare

✓ Print out enough copies of **Reproducible 1b: Love Is . . .**, found at the end of the lesson, so there is one for each child.

✓ Provide Bibles and pencils.

Love

Large Group

Bring all the children together to experience the Bible verse. Use a bell to alert the children to the large-group time.

Prepare

✓ Write on a markerboard the Bible verse: "Complete my joy by thinking the same way, having the same love, being united, and agreeing with each other" (Philippians 2:2).

✓ *Hint*: For your own reference during the activity, create a list of actions that illustrate ways that Jesus says to live. For example, Jesus says pray to God, sing a song, give a hug, and so forth. Then create a list of ways Jesus does not want us to live. For example, grumble all the time, scream at people, pout when you're upset, and so forth.

Jesus Says

- Have the children stand in a circle.

- **Say**: These next four weeks, we will be learning why Jesus was born. We will discover that Jesus came down to earth to show us how to live. Today, we are going to play a game to help us think about some of the ways that Jesus says to live.

- **Say**: In this game, I'm going to tell you some things to do. Part of the time I'll tell you "Jesus says," and part of the time I won't say it. If I tell you "Jesus says," then do what I say. If I don't tell you "Jesus says," then don't do what I say. For example, if I tell you, "Jesus says…pray to God," then show me how you pray to God. If I tell you "Grumble all the time" but don't tell you "Jesus says," then don't grumble. Got it?

- Play a few times.

- **Ask**: What are some other ways that Jesus says to act? What are ways that Jesus says not to act?

- Invite a child to be the leader and continue playing until each child has had a chance to lead.

- **Say**: Today, our Bible verse tells us to love like Jesus.

- Read together the Bible verse you prepared: "Complete my joy by thinking the same way, having the same love, being united, and agreeing with each other" (Philippians 2:2).

- **Say**: This is what it means to think and act like Jesus. When we love like Jesus, God is full of joy. Today, we are discovering ways to be like Jesus and have the same love that Jesus had for others.

- Repeat the Bible verse together.

Down to Earth: Children's Leader Guide

The Good Samaritan

- Good Samaritan is a Bible story you may have heard before. Jesus told this story to teach us how to love God and to love others.
- **Say**: Listen to this phrase: "Jesus came down to earth to show us how to love." Now repeat it after me.
- **Say**: Whenever I point to you, I'd like you to repeat that phrase.
- Read the story from the sheet, pointing at the group when indicated. The group will say together, "Jesus came down to earth to show us how to love." Have the class repeat the phrase one last time at the end of the story.
- **Ask**: What are some ways we can love God? When have you or a friend been hurt by another person's actions or words? When is it easy to show love like the Samaritan? When might have you not shown love? What are some ways that we can love others?

Prepare

✓ The leader will need a copy of **Reproducible 1c: The Good Samaritan,** found at the end of the lesson.

Making a Prayer

- **Say**: Advent is the time before Christmas. During this season, we get ready for Jesus to come down to earth. Today we have learned that Jesus came down to earth to show us how to love. We are going to write a prayer to use in our worship.
- Read what you have written on the newsprint or markerboard.
- **Ask**: Help me write a prayer by finishing the sentence, "Thank you Jesus for showing us…"? What are some ways we can show love like Jesus?
- Write down the children's responses on the newsprint or markerboard to create the prayer.
- Have an older child read Philippians 2:2.
- Light the first Advent wreath candle with a lighter or a twist of yellow tissue paper.
- **Say**: We light this first candle to remind us that Jesus loves us and we are to love others.
- Pray together the prayer that the group wrote.
- Dismiss children to their small groups.

Prepare

✓ Create a worship table with a blue or purple cloth and the Advent wreath.

✓ On a large piece of newsprint or markerboard write, "Thank you Jesus for coming down to earth to show us how to love. Thank you Jesus for showing us…"

✓ Provide a Bible and a lighter or twist of yellow tissue paper for the flame.

Love

Small Groups

Divide the children into small groups. You may organize the groups around grade levels or around readers and nonreaders. Keep the groups small, with a maximum of ten children in each group. You may need to have more than one group at each grade level.

Prepare

- ✓ Provide red and pink construction paper, markers, and scissors.
- ✓ *Tip*: Cut the construction paper in different size squares that can be folded and cut into a heart.

Young Children

- Have the children sit at tables.
- **Say**: Why did Jesus come down to earth?
- Encourage the children to share what they remember, asking questions to assist them if necessary.
- **Ask**: Do you like fun surprises?
- **Say**: We have learned today that Jesus came down to earth to show us how to love. Today, we are going to make some surprise messages for the people in our church.
- Show the children how to fold their paper square and cut on the fold to create a heart.
- Have the children cut out a lot of hearts in a variety of sizes from the construction paper.
- Encourage the children to work together and write on each heart "Jesus loves you" or other messages of love.
- When all the hearts have a message on them, gather the children as a group and go with them to various parts of the church, distributing the hearts where people will find them. You might suggest that they put hearts on some of the seats in the sanctuary or in some of the hymnals. If your church has mailboxes for staff or members, you might put hearts in the mailboxes. Let the children decide where to distribute the hearts. Then go back to the classroom.
- **Ask**: How do you think people will feel when they discover a surprise heart? How does it make you feel to leave these surprises?
- **Say**: You have reminded people that Jesus came down to earth to show us how to love. You have loved like Jesus loved. This week, find ways that you can show love to others.
- **Pray**: Thank you, God, for sending us your Son, Jesus, to show us how to love. Help us show your love to our family and friends. Amen.

Older Children

- **Ask**: Why was Jesus born?
- **Say**: Jesus came down to earth to show us how to love. We are to love like Jesus even when it is hard.
- **Ask**: Do you think it was hard for the Samaritan to show love to the man on the side of the road? Why, or why not? When the preacher and the teacher walked by the man who was hurt, why was it hard for them to show love? When is hard for you to love others?
- **Say**: When you help someone that you don't like, you are loving when it's hard. When you are helping another person even when you would rather be doing something else, you are loving when it's hard.
- **Say**: Today, we're going to practice loving like Jesus. We're going to make cards of love. Let's think of some people who might need to get a card to remember they are loved.
- Share with the class who will be receiving the cards they make.
- Give each child a piece of construction paper. Show the children how to fold their paper square and cut on the fold to create a heart.
- Have the children cut out a lot of hearts in a variety of sizes from the construction paper.
- Encourage the children to decorate their cards and write a message on the inside.
- **Say**: We too, can live like Jesus and show love to others. We will be sending your messages of love to people who need them.
- **Pray**: Loving Christ, you came down to earth to show us how to love and care for others. Show us how to love even when we don't like another person. Show us how to love even when we would rather do something else. Help us to show your love in all that we say and do this week. Amen.

Prepare

✓ Provide construction paper, pencils, scissors, crayons, and markers

✓ Before class, decide who will receive the cards. Possibilities include store clerks, church staff, homebound members, waiters and waitresses, persons in the hospital. Make arrangements for the cards to be delivered.

Love

Reproducible 1a

Same or Different?

Work with another person. Read each statement and decide whether your two answers are the same or different. Put a check under the correct heading.

	Same	Different
The color of our hair	_____	_____
Our parents' names	_____	_____
The church we attend	_____	_____
The color of our clothes	_____	_____
Our favorite Christmas cookie	_____	_____
The name of our pastor	_____	_____
Our favorite Christmas carol	_____	_____
The sport we like to play	_____	_____
The number of brothers or sisters we have	_____	_____
Our age	_____	_____
The one gift we want for Christmas	_____	_____
Whether we have a pet	_____	_____
The school we go to	_____	_____
Our favorite thing that happens at Christmas	_____	_____

Copyright © 2016 Abingdon Press • *Permission is granted to photocopy this page for local church use only.*

Reproducible 1b

Love Is...

Look up Matthew 25:35-36 in your Bible. Fill in the statement with the correct word. These are ways that Jesus teaches us to love others.

1. I was hungry and you gave me _____ to eat.

2. I was thirsty and you gave me a _____.

3. I was a stranger and you _____ me.

4. I was without clothes and you gave me _____ to wear.

5. I was sick and you took _____ of me.

6. I was in prison and you _____ me.

Answers:

1. food; 2. drink; 3. welcomed; 4. clothes; 5. care; 6. visited

Copyright © 2016 Abingdon Press • *Permission is granted to photocopy this page for local church use only.*

Reproducible 1c

The Good Samaritan
Based on Luke 10:25-37

Someone asked Jesus, "Who is my neighbor?" And Jesus told this story:

A man went down from Jerusalem to Jericho. He came across some thieves, who took off his clothes, beat him up, and left him near death. (Point to the group.)

Jesus came down to earth to show us how to love.

A little while later, a preacher was also going down that road. When he saw the injured man, he crossed over to the other side of the road and went on his way.

Jesus came down to earth to show us how to love.

Next, a teacher came along, saw the injured man, crossed over to the other side of the road, and went on his way.

Jesus came down to earth to show us how to love.

Finally a Samaritan, a man no one liked, came down the road. When he saw the injured man, he leaned down and bandaged the man's wounds. Then he placed the man on his own donkey, took him to an inn, and took care of him.

Jesus came down to earth to show us how to love.

The next day, he gave some money to the innkeeper, saying, "Take care of him, and when I return, I will pay you again if I need to."

Jesus came down to earth to show us how to love.

At the end of the story, Jesus asked, "Which one of these three acted like a neighbor?" Someone answered, "The one who showed love and cared for him." Jesus said, "Go and do likewise."

Jesus came down to earth to show us how to love.

Copyright © 2016 Abingdon Press • *Permission is granted to photocopy this page for local church use only.*

2 Be Humble

Objectives

The children will:
- Define the word *humble* and discover ways to be humble.
- Learn how Jesus shows us to be humble.
- Practice our down-to-earth mission to be humble.

Theme

Jesus came down to earth to show us how to be humble.

Bible Verse

"Instead of each person watching out for their own good, watch out for what is better for others. Adopt the attitude that was in Christ Jesus." (Philippians 2:4-5)

Focus for the Teacher

Jesus was born to poor, working-class parents in an obscure, remote village. Jesus was part of an ethnic race of minority people who have experienced persecution and genocide. Jesus lived as a refugee when his parents fled the persecution of Herod. Jesus showed us how to be humble when he ate with sinners, loved and cared for those who were persecuted, washed his disciples' feet, and died on a cross between two criminals.

To be humble means that we do not consider ourselves better than others. Paul wrote to the Philippians that we are to have the same attitude as Christ; in other words, we are to think and act like Jesus. We are to be humble and not consider ourselves better than others, because we are followers of Jesus. Having the same attitude as Christ means seeing others as Jesus sees them. It means respecting and valuing people, even those who are different from us or think differently than we do. It means thinking about others rather than ourselves.

> Like Jesus, we are to be humble.

To be humble may be an unfamiliar concept for children. This week's activities will introduce the words *humble* and *humility*. We will compare and contrast the word *humility* with its opposite, the word *pride*. Children will discover that when they think of others rather than themselves, they are being humble. We will talk about and practice our down-to-earth mission to be humble.

The best way to teach humility is to model it. Love and respect all the children in your class, and avoid favorites. Be a servant leader who grows closer to God and cares for others; who encourages others and builds their confidence; who admits being wrong and apologizes. Besides modeling humble behavior, teach humility by correcting children's poor behaviors or decisions, privately coaching them how to act, and by recognizing children when they show humility.

Down to Earth: Children's Leader Guide

Explore Interest Groups

Be sure that adult leaders are waiting when the first child arrives. Greet and welcome the children. Get the children involved in an activity that interests them and introduces the theme for the day's activities.

Cooperative Obstacle Course

- **Say**: Jesus came down to earth to show us how to be humble. Being humble means not thinking we are better than others and not being afraid to get help from others. One way we are humble is to work together.
- Encourage the children to walk through the obstacle course with you and practice the different tasks.
- **Say**: Now, instead of seeing who can run through the course the fastest, we are going to take turns with a partner to complete the course blindfolded. We will see how we have to work together.
- Divide children into teams of two. Blindfold one child in each team.
- Encourage the child who is not blindfolded to help the other child through the course.
- At the end of the course, have the children switch roles—the blindfolded and the helper—then repeat the activity until everyone has experienced both roles.
- **Ask**: What tasks were easy? What was hard? How was your partner helpful?
- **Say**: As you worked together to complete the obstacle course, you practiced what it means to be humble. We all have different strengths and abilities that are gifts from God. We can each use our gifts to work together.

Prepare

✓ Before class, create a simple obstacle course. The course might call for children to crawl under a table, bounce from one pillow to another, balance one foot on a stool, climb into a riding toy and go around a chair, walk a taped line on the floor, go down a slide, and so forth.

✓ Provide blindfolds.

God's Eye Ornament

- **Say**: Jesus came down to earth to show us how to be humble. One way we are humble is to see others the way Jesus sees them. Jesus loved and cared for everyone. We are to see others as our brothers and sisters. We are going to make a God's Eye ornament to remind us to see everyone worthy of love and care, in the same way that Jesus sees all of us.
- Give each child two wooden craft sticks, a small ball of yarn, and glue.
- Instruct the children to cross their sticks at the middle.
- Ask them to glue the sticks together. *Hint*: Use just a small amount of glue.
- Begin wrapping the yarn around the left arm.
- Wrap the yarn around the bottom arm, then up and around the right arm.

Prepare

✓ Provide for each child two wooden craft sticks, a small ball of yarn, and glue.

✓ *Hint*: Find God's Eye craft instructions on YouTube and practice making this ornament in advance, so you can demonstrate it to the children.

Be Humble

- Wrap the yarn around the top arm and overlap the piece of yarn you have left dangling.
- *Hint*: You might need to start a few ornaments to this point, particularly for younger children.
- Continue wrapping the yarn in this way – left, bottom, right, top until almost all the stick is covered.
- Help the children cut and tie off the yarn.
- Using about 6 inches of the remaining yarn, tie it into a loop.
- Glue the loop onto the top of the ornament. This is the loop that will be used to hang the ornament.
- Encourage the children to hang their ornament in class and at home on the tree.
- **Say**: Jesus teaches us to be humble. Jesus sees us and loves everyone. Jesus shows us how to see others as our brothers and sisters in Christ.

Humble Is...

- **Say**: Jesus came down to earth to show us how to be humble. Let's explore other ways to be humble.
- Give each child a copy of **Humble Is...**.
- Read together the list of words at the bottom of the puzzle.
- **Say**: All these words help us understand the word *humble*. These words are hidden in the puzzle. The words might be up, down, across, backward, or diagonal. When you find a word, circle it. This activity will give us more ideas about what Jesus taught us about being humble.

Prepare

✓ Provide each child a copy of **Reproducible 2a: Humble Is...** found at the end of the lesson.

✓ Provide pencils.

Answer Key:

[word search puzzle grid with circled answers]

Down to Earth: Children's Leader Guide

Acts of Kindness

- **Say**: Today's Bible verse tells us to think about others rather than ourselves.
- **Read the Bible verse again:** "Instead of each person watching out for their own good, watch out for what is better for others. Adopt the attitude that was in Christ Jesus" (Philippians 2:4-5).
- **Say**: When we are kind, we think about the other person. Acts of kindness are small acts that are done with no motive and, usually, without recognition.
- **Ask**: What are some ways that you can be kind to another person?
- **Say**: I have a basket of papers that give ways to show kindness to someone. Each child will draw a paper and do the act of kindness to someone in the room.
- Encourage the children to participate. If needed, help them complete the act of kindness sometime during the session.
- **Say**: Feel free to take this card or draw another card and do the act of kindness this week.

Prepare

✓ Before class, cut apart the cards or strips of paper from **Reproducible 2b: Acts of Kindness,** found at the end of the lesson. Place the cards or paper strips in a basket, face down. Depending on how many children are in your group, you may want to cut apart multiple copies of the sheet.

Be Humble

Large Group

Bring all the children together to experience the Bible study. Use a bell to alert the children to the large-group time.

Prepare

✓ Write on a markerboard the Bible verse: "Instead of each person watching out for their own good, watch out for what is better for others. Adopt the attitude that was in Christ Jesus" (Philippians 2:4-5).

✓ Write on a nametag a character trait that exemplifies humility, such as meek, helpful, kind, caring, gentle, and so forth. You will need a nametag for each person in the class. If needed, you can duplicate words.

Jesus Shows Us How to Be Humble

- **Ask**: Why did Jesus come down to earth? What are some ways you have shown love this past week?
- Encourage children to share.
- **Say**: We learned that Jesus came down to earth to show us how to love. We practiced ways that we can show love like Jesus. Today's Bible verse reminds us that Jesus came down to earth to show us how to be humble.
- Read together the Bible verse from the markerboard: "Instead of each person watching out for their own good, watch out for what is better for others. Adopt the attitude that was in Christ Jesus" (Philippians 2:4-5).
- **Say**: When we work together or when we love everyone or when we are kind to others, we have the same attitude as Jesus. We are being humble. Let's discover more ways that we can be humble.
- Read a word on a nametag.
- **Ask**: How can you be [the word on the nametag]?
- Give each child a nametag.
- **Say**: Take the nametag and put it on. You have been given a new name. You have adopted a new attitude. Today and this week, practice being humble—adopt the same attitude as Jesus.
- Repeat the Bible verse together.

Prepare

✓ Provide a markerboard and marker.

✓ Before class, write each incomplete sentence on the markerboard.

Choose to be Humble

- **Say**: As followers of Jesus, we are to adopt the same attitude as Jesus. We are to be humble.
- **Ask**: What are some ways you can be humble this week?
- **Say**: We are going to write a litany to use in our worship. I will read a sentence and we will work together to complete the sentence showing how we can be humble.
- Encourage the children to complete each sentence. *Hint*: Try to help the children write positive statements (We will…) rather than negative statements (We will not…).
    - o   At home, we will _____.
    - o   At school, we will _____.
    - o   When we are with our friends, we will _____.
    - o   If we see someone who needs help, we will _____.

Down to Earth: Children's Leader Guide

Humility or Pride

- Divide the children into groups of three or four. Be sure that there are older and younger children in each group.
- **Say**: Jesus came down to earth to show us *humility*, which means being humble. One of the ways we are humble is to work together and depend on one another. The word *pride* is the opposite of humility. When you are full of pride, you are not being humble. You are thinking of yourself. I'm going to read a statement, and the group can decide if it shows being humble or being full of pride. If it shows how to be humble, go and stand under the sign that says "Humility." If the statement shows how to be full of pride, go and stand under the sign that says "Pride."
- Read the following statements and give time for the group to decide whether it illustrates humility or pride. Applaud the groups when they are correct, and guide the groups when they are unsure or incorrect.
    - You work together on a project recognizing that everyone can contribute or help complete the project.
    - You say to a classmate, "I'm better than you!"
    - You only care about yourself.
    - You know that people matter to God, so you treat them with dignity and respect.
    - You think about what others think or feel.
    - You don't brag about yourself. Instead you brag about others: "Did you see her art project? It is amazing!" or "You can do it."
    - You go around talking about others behind their back.
    - You are considerate of others.
    - You pout or cry when you don't get what you want.
    - You tell others thank you. You tell others how much you appreciate them.
    - You hate to be told what to do and demand your own way.
    - You know that you make mistakes and say, "I'm sorry."
    - You help others without being asked.
    - Others don't like to be around you because you talk about yourself and put others down.
    - Others like being around you because you make them feel loved.

Prepare

✓ Before class, create two posters. On one poster write the word *Humility*, and on the other poster write the word *Pride*. Hang the posters on opposite sides of the room.

Be Humble

Prepare

✓ Before class, write on a poster or paper, "We adopt the same attitude as Jesus. We choose to be humble." Put the poster in a box and wrap it as a Christmas gift. Make the gift a bit complicated to unwrap, such as by wrapping boxes within boxes.

✓ Hang the litany that the class wrote in the worship area.

✓ Provide the Christmas gift, a DVD player, a DVD of Christmas carols, a Bible, the Advent wreath, and a lighter or twist of yellow tissue paper for the candle.

Down-to-Earth Mission to Be Humble

- Have the children move to the worship area and sit in a circle.
- **Say**: During Advent, we prepare for Jesus to come down to earth. We have learned that Jesus came down to earth to show us how to be humble. Today I have a Christmas gift. We're going to work together to unwrap it. When the music is playing, pass it around the circle. When the music stops, the child holding the gift can do one thing to begin unwrapping it. When the music starts again, pass the gift around the circle some more.
- Start playing a Christmas carol and start the gift around the circle. Continue until the gift is unwrapped.
- **Ask**: What does the gift say?
- Invite the children to read the message together: "We adopt the same attitude as Jesus. We choose to be humble."
- **Say**: Jesus is a gift to us. Jesus came down to earth to show us how to live. Today, we have learned how to be humble like Jesus.
- Light the second Advent wreath candle.
- **Say**: We light the second candle to remind us that we are to think of others. We are to be humble.
- Pray together the litany that the group wrote, saying together after each sentence, "We choose to be humble."
- Dismiss children to their small groups.

Small Groups

Divide the children into small groups. You may organize the groups around grade levels or around readers and nonreaders. Keep the groups small, with a maximum of ten children in each group. You may need to have more than one group at each grade level.

Young Children

- **Say**: Today, we have talked about ways that Jesus shows us how to think of others. Jesus shows us how to be humble. There are many people who do jobs that we may not notice or thank them for.
- **Ask**: Who helps you at home? at church? at school? in your neighborhood? (This could be parent, teacher, janitor, librarian.)
- **Say**: Oftentimes we forget to thank those who help us. One way we can be humble is to thank others. We are going to make some thank-you cards.
- Give each child a sheet of card stock paper.
- Tell the children to fold their paper in half, matching short side against short side.
- Fold the paper again in half the other way, to make a card.
- Encourage the children to write *Thank You* on the front and draw a picture either on the front or the inside of the card.
- Help the children write a message on the inside of the card and sign their name.
- **Say**: Take this card with you. Remember to give the card to a person this week.
- Have the children stand in a circle and tell who they are thankful for.
- **Pray**: Loving Jesus, thank you for coming down to earth to show us how to be humble. Thank you for these people who help us. Remind us to be kind and to thank others. Amen.

Prepare

✓ Provide white card stock paper, colored pencils, and crayons.

Prepare

✓ Provide a copy of **Reproducible 2c: I Can Give,** found at the end of the lesson.

✓ Provide pens or pencils.

Older Children

- **Ask**: What is the one gift you want to receive this Christmas?
- **Say**: Christmas is more than wanting gifts; it is also giving to others. Jesus shows us how to be humble. Jesus shows us how to think of others, not just ourselves.
- **Ask**: What can you do to be humble at home? at school? at church? in your neighborhood?
- Encourage children to be creative with their answers. For example: clean out your toys and donate gently-used toys to a shelter; do a chore without being asked; thank a sales clerk; help a neighbor with a chore; make cookies for an elderly friend; compliment someone; put change in a parking meter; volunteer at a food bank.
- **Say**: You are going to create a calendar and identify ways to be humble this week.
- Give each child a copy of **I Can Give**.
- Have the children write one way they plan to be humble for each day of the week.
- If needed, help children come up with an idea. Make sure it's something that the children can actually accomplish.
- **Say**: Take your calendar home and hang it in your room or on your refrigerator. Be sure that you complete the task to be humble each day. I look forward to hearing your stories next week about being humble.
- Have the children form a circle. Invite each of them to share one way they plan to be humble this week.
- **Pray**: Awesome God, we thank you that your Son, Jesus Christ, came down to earth to show us how to be humble. Help us this week to be humble. Thank you for [name each child in the group]. Help all of us this week to be humble. Amen.

Down to Earth: Children's Leader Guide

Reproducible 2a

Humble Is...

Find the words hidden in the puzzle. The words will be up, down, across, backward, or diagonal.

```
C T H P K G J Y S Q G R E E Z
O Y H I H S F G Q B N T L T C
U L N O C O O P E R A T I V E
R D U D U D J E O N N A G J S
T F H F W G L U O E P D N M F
E Y J X P S H I G O K K I U G
O M F Y O L S T L D O F R D N
U Y O N B S E O F L K M A B W
S G F D A N G H Z U R S C T C
B W W P E I H S I F L E S N U
H B M G Z S P R L O N U T Y O
D O K E A R T M G B P U Q C E
C Z G Q K A G E L T Z S I P F
W R O P K J V E X F U D Q I C
P O L I T E R K U U Z I H K H
```

APOLOGIZE	GENTLE	POLITE
CARING	HELPFUL	THOUGHTFUL
COMPASSIONATE	KIND	UNSELFISH
COOPERATIVE	MEEK	
COURTEOUS	MODEST	

Copyright © 2016 Abingdon Press • Permission is granted to photocopy this page for local church use only.

Reproducible 2b

Acts of Kindness

- -

Hug a friend and tell them why you like them.

- -

Tell someone you are sorry for something you did.

- -

Be kind to someone.

- -

Find a partner and pick up trash together.

- -

Talk to someone new in the class or
someone you don't know very well.

- -

Go to someone in the room and smile at them.

- -

Hold the door or a chair for someone.

- -

Copyright © 2016 Abingdon Press • Permission is granted to photocopy this page for local church use only.

Reproducible 2c

I Can Give

SUNDAY	
MONDAY	
TUESDAY	
WEDNESDAY	
THURSDAY	
FRIDAY	
SATURDAY	

Copyright © 2016 Abingdon Press • *Permission is granted to photocopy this page for local church use only.*

3 Serve

Objectives
The children will:
- Discover the importance of Joseph's dream.
- Explore how we live like Jesus by serving others.
- Practice our down-to-earth mission to serve others.

Theme
Jesus came down to earth to show us how to serve others.

Bible Verse
"When Joseph woke up, he did just as an angel from God commanded and took Mary as his wife." (Matthew 1:24)

Focus for the Teacher

Joseph, when he discovered that Mary was pregnant, was going to call off the marriage quietly. He did not want to expose her to public disgrace that might have resulted in Mary being stoned to death. However, in a dream God told Joseph to not be afraid but to take Mary as his wife. The child Mary was carrying was conceived by the Holy Spirit, and his name would be Jesus. Joseph received a God-size dream—a divine intervention that required Joseph to take responsibility to follow and serve God. Knowing that God was with him, Joseph woke and did as God commanded.

Throughout his life, Jesus showed us how to serve. On his last night with his disciples, Jesus took a towel and washed the disciples' feet, taking the role of a servant. We too, are to serve others. We are to be servants who take compassionate action.

This week's lesson will explore Joseph's dream and some of the ways we too can follow Jesus by serving others. Children can understand with guidance how Christmas isn't only a time of receiving gifts but is also a time to give by serving others. The children will have an opportunity to discover how to serve others and to practice serving others.

> Like Jesus, we serve others.

At the end of the session, the children will be doing a low-cost service project for a family member. This reinforces that our service begins at home and that serving others comes from the heart.

Think about the children in your group, your congregation, and your neighborhood. What are ways that children serve at church? at school? in their neighborhood? List some ways that children might serve others this Christmas.

Down to Earth: Children's Leader Guide

Explore Interest Groups

Be sure that adult leaders are waiting when the first child arrives. Greet and welcome the children. Get the children involved in an activity that interests them and introduces the theme for the day's activities.

Follow Me

- Choose a leader. Have the other children line up behind the leader.
- Tell the leader to lead the children around the playing area. Encourage the leader to walk in different ways (small steps, large steps, march, crawl . . .) and to use different movements (fly like an airplane, swing the arms, pat the head . . .).
- The children in the line are to follow the leader.
- Invite another child to be the leader and continue playing.
- **Say**: Today, we are going to hear a story about how Joseph followed God. We are also going to discover how Jesus came down to earth to serve others. We will practice following God as we serve others.

Prepare

✓ Provide a large playing area.

My Dad

- Give each child a sheet of paper.
- Invite the children to draw a picture of their father or some other important man in their lives.
- Encourage the children to add words or pictures about the person. These can be words that describe him (funny, loving, protective, hard-working, patient, gentle . . .) or that show what they enjoy doing with him. You may need to help younger children write their words.
- Invite the children to share their pictures.
- **Say**: Today, we are going to hear a story about Jesus' earthly father, Joseph.

Prepare

✓ Provide white sheets of paper, crayons, and colored pencils.

✓ *Hint*: If you have children in your class who may not know their father or have a difficult relationship with their father, help them think about a man in their life who is like a father to them.

Serve

Prepare

✓ Provide for each child six-inch-long, red and white pipe cleaners (also called a chenille stem).

✓ Find a picture of a shepherd's crook, also known as a shepherd's staff.

Candy Cane Ornament

- **Say**: Today, we are going to learn about Joseph, Jesus' earthly father. Joseph was a carpenter, but sometimes you see pictures of Joseph carrying a shepherd's crook. (You might want to show the children a shepherd's crook.) A shepherd's crook can be used to keep your balance when walking along mountainous or uneven terrain and to pull a sheep out of danger. It is also a symbol to remind us to care for others. Today we are going to make a candy cane ornament that is shaped like a shepherd's crook.

- Give each child one red and one white pipe cleaner.

- Show the children how to twist the pipe cleaners together. If possible, make the stripes of the combined red-and-white stem neatly spaced.

- Curl the top into a hook.

- Encourage the children to hang their ornament on the tree.

- **Say**: Jesus came down to earth to show us how to serve others. The candy cane ornament looks like a shepherd's crook. It reminds us to care for others. Today, we are going to practice ways that we can care for and serve others.

Prepare

✓ Provide copies of **Reproducible 3a: Serving Is...**, found at the end of the lesson.

✓ Provide Bibles and pencils.

Serving Is...

- **Say**: Today, we will learn how Jesus came down to earth to show us how to serve others.

- Pair children into groups of two or three. Be sure to pair younger children with older children.

- Give each child a Bible, a pencil, and a copy of the puzzle **Serving Is...**.

- Encourage the children to look up the Bible verse and to fill in the blanks. Show the children how to write their answer in the crossword puzzle. (Wording is based on the Common English Bible translation, but children should be able to fill in words from other translations.)

- **Say**: Jesus teaches us how to serve others.

- **Ask**: What are some ways that we can serve others?

- Encourage the children to share their ideas. Be sure to discuss how the words in the crossword puzzle tell us ways that we can serve.

Down to Earth: Children's Leader Guide

Large Group

Bring all the children together to experience the Bible study. Use a bell to alert the children to the large-group time.

Dream Bubbles

- **Ask**: Why did Jesus come down to earth? What are some ways that you have loved others this week? What are some ways that you have been humble this week?
- Encourage children to share.
- **Say**: Today, we are going to learn how Jesus came down to earth to show us how to serve.
- Give each child a copy of **Dream Bubbles**.
- **Ask**: What is a dream?
- **Say**: Dreams are what we think about when we are asleep. Dreams might be about people or objects, thoughts or ideas, or even how we are feeling. On your paper, draw pictures or write words in the bubbles of the best dream you can imagine.
- Invite the children to share their dreams.

Prepare

✓ Provide copies of **Reproducible 3b: Dream Bubbles**, found at the end of the lesson.

✓ Provide crayons and colored pencils.

Joseph's Story

- **Ask**: Who was Jesus' earthly father? Who was Jesus' mother?
- **Say**: Today, we are going to hear a story about Joseph's dream.
- Ask the reader to tell the story of Joseph's dream from the handout.
- **Ask**: What did God tell Joseph? How do you think Joseph felt? What do you think it was like for Joseph to be Jesus' earthly father?
- Read together the Bible verse from your markerboard: "When Joseph woke up, he did just as an angel from God commanded and took Mary as his wife" (Matthew 1:24).
- **Say**: Joseph followed God. He took Mary as his wife. They became Jesus' parents.

Prepare

✓ Write on a markerboard the Bible verse: "When Joseph woke up, he did just as an angel from God commanded and took Mary as his wife" (Matthew 1:24).

✓ Ask a good reader from your class to read the story of Joseph from **Reproducible 3c: Joseph's Story**, found at the end of the lesson.

Serve

Prepare

✓ On the markerboard, create a template for a cinquain poem, which will be described in the lesson. On the first row, write the word *Serve*. On the second row, draw two lines; on the third row draw three lines; on the fourth row draw four lines; and on the fifth row draw one line.

✓ Provide the Advent wreath and a lighter or twist of yellow tissue paper.

Down-to-Earth Mission to Serve

- Have the children move to the worship area and sit in a circle.

- **Ask**: What are some ways that you serve others at home? in your church? in your community?

- Encourage children to share their stories. Affirm the different ways children serve others. Hint: Write down some key words and phrases that the children share.

- **Say**: Today, we are going to write a prayer. Our prayer will be a five-line poem called a cinquain.
    - The first line is one word, Serve, which is the title of the poem.
    - The second line contains two words that describe the title.
    - The third line has three words that tell the reader more about the subject of the poem or shows action. Many times these action words end with "ing."
    - The fourth line has four words that show emotions about the subject of the poem or a phrase about the subject.
    - The fifth line is one word that is a synonym of the title or is very similar to it.

- As a group, work together to write the poem. Refer back to the thoughts of the children for key words and phrases. If you have a large group, you may choose to divide the class and work in smaller groups to create several different poems.

- Here is a sample cinquain that you may want to share with the group:
    - Serve
    - Follow God
    - Listening, forgiving, sharing
    - A gift to others
    - Love

- Gather the children around the worship table.

- **Ask**: Why did Jesus come down to earth?

- Encourage children to share their answers.

- **Say**: We have learned how to love like Jesus. (Light the first Advent wreath candle.) We have practiced how to be humble like Jesus. (Light the second Advent wreath candle.) Today, we have talked about ways to serve like Jesus. (Light the third Advent wreath candle.)

- Pray together the poem that the group wrote.

- Dismiss children to their small groups.

Down to Earth: Children's Leader Guide

We Can Serve

- **Say**: Joseph served God by following the messenger's instructions. Today, we are going to discover that Jesus came down to earth to show us how to serve others. One of the greatest gifts that we can give is to serve others.

- **Ask**: What does it mean to serve others?

- Encourage the children to share their answers. Hint: Use the different words in the crossword puzzle "Serving Is. . ." to talk about what it means to serve others.

- **Say**: We have many opportunities to serve others every day. We are going to play a game about the ways we serve.

- Choose one child to stand in the center of the circle of chairs, and have the rest of the children sit in the chairs.

- Explain the following rules to the children:

- The person in the center will say one way that they have served another person such as "I made a get-well card for someone," or "I gave clothes that don't fit me anymore to someone else," or "I read a book to my younger sister."

- Every person in the circle for whom that statement is true must get up and find a new seat, while the person in the middle tries to get a seat also.

- The person left standing becomes the next leader.

- Play several times.

Prepare

✓ Form a circle of chairs facing inward, using one chair fewer than the number of children in your class.

Serve

Small Groups

Divide the children into small groups. You may organize the groups around grade levels or around readers and nonreaders. Keep the groups small, with a maximum of ten children in each group. You may need to have more than one group at each grade level..

✓ Provide long sheets of butcher paper, pencils, scissors, and crayons.

✓ Provide a note or send an e-mail after class asking parents to help their children send their hugs to a family member they will not see this Christmas.

Young Children

- **Ask**: Why did Jesus come down to earth?
- Encourage children to share their answers.
- **Say**: Last week, we learned how to be humble like Jesus. You made a thank-you card to give someone.
- **Ask**: Who did you give your card to?
- **Say**: Today, we learned that Jesus came down to earth to show us how to serve others.
- **Ask**: What are some ways that you can serve at home?
- **Say**: Serving comes from the heart. Serving shows others how much we care about them. One of the best ways I know to show that you care is with a hug.
- **Ask**: Who are you going to see this Christmas? Who will you not get to see?
- **Say**: We are going to make a hug that you can send to your grandparents, to a favorite aunt or uncle, or to someone that you will not get to see this Christmas.
- Pair the children.
- Give each pair two long sheets of butcher paper.
- One child is to lie on their back with their head and outstretched arms on the paper.
- Tell the partner to trace around the child's head and arms.
- Swap and let the other child lay on the blank sheet of paper with their partner tracing around their head and outstretched arms.
- Tell the children to cut out their head and arms.
- Show how the person who receives the hug can wrap the arms around themselves.
- Encourage the children to decorate their hug.
- **Say**: Take your hug home and ask your parents to help you mail your hug.
- **Say**: Another way we serve is to pray for others.
- Invite the children to stand in a circle and hold hands.
- **Say**: I'm going to start the prayer. When I'm finished, I will gently squeeze the hand of the next person in the circle. Feel free to offer a prayer. When you finish or if you wish to pass, gently squeeze the person's hand next to you.
- Continue praying around the circle.
- **Say**: All God's children said, "Amen."

Older Children

- **Ask**: Why did Jesus come down to earth?
- Encourage children to share their answers.
- **Say**: Last week, we thought about others rather than ourselves. You created a calendar showing how you would be humble by giving to others.
- **Ask**: What were some ways that you were humble last week?
- **Say**: Today, we learned that Jesus came down to earth to show us how to serve others. Serving comes from the heart. We can serve at home. We can serve by showing our parents that we care.
- **Ask**: What things can you do around the house that will help your parents? What can you do to show your parents that you love them?
- Write the children's answers on the markerboard.
- **Say**: These are ways that we can serve at home. We are going to make a coupon book that you can give to your parents for Christmas. Your mother and father will be able to redeem their coupons for your service. For example, one coupon might be to clean your room or give your mother a hug. (Add ideas that the children have already shared.)
- Give each child several colored squares of paper and a loose-leaf binder ring.
- Invite the children to write one coupon per square. They may choose to decorate their coupons.
- Once they have created 6-8 coupons, have them stack the squares together and punch a hole in the upper corner.
- Fasten the squares together with a loose-leaf binder ring.
- **Say**: Take your coupon book home and give it to your parents on Christmas. Your parents can redeem their coupons. You can serve at home throughout the year.
- **Say**: Another way we serve is to pray for others. Who do you want to pray for today?
- List the names of persons or concerns on the markerboard.
- **Say**: I'm going to pray for a person we have listed. After I say a prayer for some of the people you named, I will say "Lord, in your mercy" and you will respond, "Hear our prayer." Hint: You may want to group names of people such as, "Thank you God for our friends [naming different friends of the children]" and so forth.
- Pray together for the different people the children named.

Prepare

✓ Provide different-colored squares of cardstock paper, pens, colored pencils or markers, a hole punch, loose-leaf binder rings, and a markerboard.

Serve

Reproducible 3a

Serving Is...

Look up each Bible verse and fill in the blank. Write your answer in the correct box on the puzzle.

Down
1. The Good Samaritan took _____ of him. (Luke 10:35)
2. "_____ and understand." (Matthew 15:10)
3. "God has come to _____ his people." (Luke 7:16)
4. "Come _____ me." (Matthew 4:19)
5. "Whoever has two shirts must _____ with the one who has none." (Luke 3:11)

Across
4. "If you _____ others."(Matthew 6:14)
6. "_____ like this." (Matthew 6:9)
7. "You must _____ your neighbor." (Matthew 22:39)

Answers:
Down: 1. Care 2. Listen 3. Help 4. Follow 5. Share **Across:** 4. Forgive 6. Pray 7. Love

Copyright © 2016 Abingdon Press • *Permission is granted to photocopy this page for local church use only.*

Reproducible 3b

Dream Bubbles

Copyright © 2016 Abingdon Press • *Permission is granted to photocopy this page for local church use only.*

Joseph's Story
Based on Matthew 1:18-25

Hello, I'm Joseph! I live and work in Nazareth. I enjoy working with my hands and make chairs, cabinets, tables, and other pieces of furniture out of wood. I also make wooden plows, wheelbarrows, and wagons for the farmers. In my spare time, I like to make wooden toys for children. What wooden toys do you like?

I'm engaged to Mary. She's a beautiful young woman. I can't wait till we're married and have children.

Yesterday when I was talking with Mary, she told me she's going to have a baby, but it's not our baby. I do love Mary, and I don't want her to be hurt. I thought maybe I should quietly call off the engagement.

Then last night I had a dream. Do you have dreams? Mine was amazing! God sent a messenger who told me not to be afraid. The messenger told me to take Mary as my wife, just as we had planned. The messenger said that Mary's baby is God's own Son, and we are to name him Jesus! That's not all. Our son Jesus will show everyone how to love, how to be humble, and how to serve!

I've decided that I'm going to follow God! I'll serve God and take Mary as my wife! I'll be the father of Jesus! I can't wait to love and take care of Jesus as he grows up. I'll teach him how to be a carpenter and make beautiful things out of wood. I'll tell him stories about God and teach him the Ten Commandments.

I can't wait for Jesus to come down to earth!

4 Be Grateful

Objectives

The children will:
- Discover how Mary obeyed and said yes to God.
- Learn the word *gratitude* and learn that when we are grateful, we say yes to God.
- Explore ways that we can be grateful.
- Celebrate that Jesus came down to earth.

Theme

Jesus came down to earth to show us how to be grateful.

Bible Verse

"As for children, obey your parents in the Lord, because it is right." (Ephesians 6:1)

Focus for the Teacher

Children learn how to obey their parents, their teachers, and other adults in their lives. Often, children experience obedience as following a list of rules or consequences for behavior. But our obedience to God is different from that. It is saying yes. It is aligning ourselves with God. It is allowing God to work in and through us to fulfill God's purposes.

How can we do these things? First, we acknowledge that God's grace has been and will continue to transform us. Second, we trust that God is working on our behalf for God's good purposes. Third, even when trusting is messy or difficult, it's our way of being grateful and allowing God to work in our hearts and our lives.

This week we'll explore our obedience to God with a focus on Mary's gratitude. Even though Mary was young, unwed, and could face shame and death for being pregnant, she said yes to God. She allowed God to work in her to fulfill God's purpose of bringing Jesus down to earth. In Mary's song of praise, known as the Magnificat, she expressed her gratitude. When Mary was able to express her thanks, she was able to put her full trust in God.

> Like Jesus, we can be grateful.

Children can experience some of the ways in which Mary said yes to God. Like Mary, children can give thanks to God and be grateful. Older children will be able to relate to being grateful even when life is difficult. We will practice our down-to-earth mission to be grateful by giving a birthday party for Jesus.

Create a list identifying what you are grateful for. Say a prayer of thanksgiving for each child and the way he or she has inspired you this Advent. Think about the children, their families, and your congregation, then list some of the things the children can be grateful for.

Down to Earth: Children's Leader Guide

Explore Interest Groups

Be sure that adult leaders are waiting when the first child arrives. Greet and welcome the children. Get the children involved in an activity that interests them and introduces the theme for the day's activities.

Gratitude Chain

- **Say**: Jesus came down to earth to show us how to be grateful. Another way of saying this is being thankful.
- **Ask**: What are you thankful for? Who in your life are you grateful for?
- Give each child several strips of red and green paper and a marker.
- Encourage children to write or draw what they are thankful for. Put one idea on each strip of paper.
- Show the children how to create a loop, closing it off with tape or a stapler.
- Then show the children how to create another loop from a paper strip and thread the second loop through the first loop to connect to create a chain.
- Continue to connect the strips of paper until the group has several long chains.
- Help the children hang the chain in the worship area.
- **Say**: One of the things we are grateful for is the gift of Jesus. He was born on Christmas to show us how to love, how to be humble, how to serve, and how to be grateful.

Prepare
✓ Provide red and green strips of construction paper, markers, and tape or staplers.

Grateful T-shirt

- **Ask**: What does it mean to be grateful?
- **Say**: Another word for grateful is *thankful*.
- **Ask**: How we can tell others to be thankful?
- Encourage the children to share their answers.
- Give each child a copy of the handout Grateful T-shirt.
- Invite the children to design their T-Shirt. Use different colors, shapes, pictures, and words to create a slogan or a design for your T-shirt, reminding others to be grateful.
- When the T-shirts are complete, invite the children to share their designs.
- **Say**: Jesus came down to show us how to be grateful.

Prepare
✓ Provide copies of **Reproducible 4a: Grateful T-shirt,** found at the end of this lesson.

✓ Provide crayons and colored pencils.

Be Grateful 53

Prepare

✓ Provide colored index cards and pencils.

Prayer Cards

- **Say**: Jesus came down to earth to show us how to be grateful. One of the ways we are grateful is to pray. We can tell God what we are thankful for. We can tell God who we are grateful for. We can pray anytime and anywhere. We can thank God for a beautiful sunset. We can thank God for our parents. Today we are going to make some prayer reminders.

- Give each child several index cards.

- Have each child write the word PRAY in large letters on each card.

- Encourage the children to decorate their cards.

- **Say**: When you take these cards home, put them around your house in places where you will see them frequently. When you see a card, take a moment and say a prayer. The prayer doesn't need to be long or complicated. It can be as simple as "God, thank you for this day." Remember, we can pray about anything!

Prepare

✓ For each child, bring two popsicle sticks and two six-inch lengths of string.

✓ For the group, bring colored markers, white paper, several pairs of scissors, and glue.

Joseph and Mary Ornaments

- **Say**: Christmas is the day that we celebrate Jesus' birth. We are very grateful that Jesus came down to earth to show us how to love, how to be humble, how to serve, and how to be grateful.

- **Ask**: What does grateful mean? What are you thankful for?

- **Say**: We are going to make Mary and Joseph ornaments to remind us that on Christmas, Jesus came down to earth to show us how to be grateful.

- Pass out two popsicle sticks and two six-inch lengths of string to each child. Invite the children to create a Mary ornament and a Joseph ornament by decorating the popsicle sticks with markers and (if desired) with paper shapes that are glued on to the sticks.

- When the children are finished, they can glue a loop of string to each ornament so it can be hung on a Christmas tree.

- **Say**: Today, we are going to be grateful. We are going to celebrate Jesus' birth.

Down to Earth: Children's Leader Guide

Large Group

Bring all the children together to experience the Bible study. Use a bell to alert the children to the large-group time.

Yes or No?

- Invite the children to sit in a circle.
- **Say**: We're going to play a game. One child will be the leader. The leader will think of an object. The object will need to be something you can see in this room. The rest of the group will ask the leader questions and try to guess the object. However, the group can only ask questions that can be answered with *yes* or *no*.
- Name one child to be the leader.
- Play until the group has identified the object.
- The child who guessed the object correctly becomes the leader.
- Continue playing.
- **Say**: Today we're going to hear a story about Mary, Jesus' mother. We will learn whether Mary said yes or no to God.

Thank You, God

- **Ask**: What are some different ways that we can express our gratitude—our thanks to God?
- **Say**: Prayer is one way we express our thanks to God. When we pray, we talk to God but we also listen. We often think of folding our hands together and bowing our heads when we pray. That's okay, but there are many other prayer positions. In fact, there is no wrong way to pray. Right now we are going to pray in several different ways. I will begin by naming a prayer position. Once everyone is in position, I will say a short prayer. We will repeat the activity several times.
- Lead the children in prayer, giving the following prayer positions and the corresponding prayers.
  o Head bowed and hands folded: God, we thank you that we can pray to you about anything.
  o Hands raised high in the air: God, we thank you that we can pray when we are joyful and excited.
  o Shoulders slumped, sad face: God, we thank you that you hear our prayers when we are sad.
  o Kneeling: God, help us remember to talk with you often.
  o Sports huddle: God, we thank you that we can pray to you wherever we are.
  o Standing, hands spread out to the side: God, we thank you that we can pray to you about anything!
  o Sitting: God, we thank you for hearing our prayers. Amen.

Be Grateful

Prepare

✓ The leader will need a copy of **Reproducible 4b: Say Yes, Mary!**, found at the end of the lesson.

✓ Write this Bible verse on a markerboard: "As for children, obey your parents in the Lord, because it is right" (Ephesians 6:1).

Say Yes, Mary!

- **Say**: I'm going to read a story about Mary, Jesus' mother. Whenever I pause in the story, you are to stand up and shout, "Say yes, Mary!"
- Allow the children to practice standing and shouting, "Say yes, Mary!"
- Read the story pausing at the end of each phrase so that children can stand and shout.
- **Ask**: Did Mary say yes or no to God? Do you think it was hard or easy for Mary to say yes? Why?
- **Read together the Bible verse**: "As for children, obey your parents in the Lord, because it is right" (Ephesians 6:1).
- **Say**: Mary obeyed God, because she knew that God was with her. Mary thanked God for choosing her to be Jesus' mother. Mary thanked God for Jesus, who would come down to earth to show us how to love, be humble, serve, and be grateful.
- **Ask**: What does it mean to be grateful?
- **Say**: When we are grateful we give thanks to God. We appreciate people who are in our lives. We know that God is always with us. When we are grateful, we follow God. We say yes to God.
- **Ask**: What are you grateful and thankful for?
  o Encourage children to share their answers.
- Encourage children to write or draw their thoughts in the space provided. Invite children to share their ideas.
- **Say**: Finally, Jesus didn't just tell the disciples to love others; he showed them how to serve others.
- Have the children sit in groups of four or six.
- Give a child in each group a bottle of hand sanitizer.
- Encourage the child to wash their neighbor's hands.
- Tell the child to pass the bottle of hand sanitizer to their neighbor.
- Continue around the circle till everyone has had a chance to wash another's hands.
- Invite the children to turn to John 13 in their Bibles. Older children can help younger children.
- Invite a confident reader to read John 13:4-5 and another child to read John 13:12-14.
- **Say:** In Jesus' days, people wore sandals. After walking all day, the disciples' feet were dusty and dirty. Usually a servant washed the guest's feet. However, this time Jesus washed the disciples' feet. They couldn't imagine that Jesus, their leader, would wash their feet. We are to serve others just as Jesus served his disciples by washing their feet.
- **Ask**: What are some ways we can serve others?
- Encourage children to write or draw their thoughts in the space provided. Invite children to share their ideas

Down-to-Earth Mission to Be Grateful

- Have the children move to the worship area and sit in a circle.
- **Ask**: What do you and your family do on Christmas day?
- Encourage children to share their answers.
- **Say**: Christmas is a day when we celebrate. It is usually a day when we are full of joy! Christmas is a day when we are grateful and give thanks that Jesus was born!
- **Ask**: Why did Jesus come down to earth?
- **Say**: Yes, Jesus came down to earth to show us how to love, to be humble, to serve, and to be grateful. Today we are going to express our gratitude by having a birthday party for Jesus! We are going to celebrate that Jesus came down to earth.
- Invite an older child to read Luke 2:1-7
- Sing "Away in a Manger."
- Hold up a cupcake with a candle. Sing "Happy Birthday" to Jesus.
- Pass out the cupcakes and cups of juice.
- **Ask**: Why are you thankful for Jesus?
- Encourage children to share their answers.
- Give each child a glow stick or a glow bracelet. Turn the lights down.
- **Say**: These past four weeks, we have learned how to love like Jesus. (Light the first Advent wreath candle.) We have practiced how to be humble like Jesus. (Light the second Advent wreath candle.) We have served like Jesus. (Light the third Advent wreath candle.) Today, we have expressed our gratitude like Jesus. (Light the fourth Advent wreath candle.)
- Sing "Silent Night."
- Dismiss children to their small groups.

Prepare

✓ Before class, decorate the worship area with birthday decorations

✓ Provide the gratitude chain that the children created earlier, in addition to cupcakes, napkins, cups of juice, glow sticks or bracelets, Advent wreath, and lighter or twist of yellow tissue paper.

✓ Leader will need a Bible and a hymnal. You can choose to sing a capella, use a YouTube video or CD, or ask a volunteer to play the hymns.

Be Grateful

Small Groups

Divide the children into small groups. You may organize the groups around grade levels or around readers and nonreaders. Keep the groups small, with a maximum of ten children in each group. You may need to have more than one group at each grade level.

Prepare

✓ Before class, cut a sheet of paper into fourths. In large, bold letters, write *Love* on one piece of paper; *Be Humble* on another piece; *Serve* on another piece; and *Be Grateful* on the last piece. Fold the pieces of paper and place them in a basket.

✓ *Optional*: Take a group picture to send to the children for Christmas. It is also a good time to thank them for being in your class.

Young Children

- **Say**: This is our last week. We have learned why Jesus came down to earth.

- **Ask**: What are some of the things Jesus taught us when he came down to earth?

- Encourage children to share their answers.

- **Say**: I'm going to pass this basket around the circle. Take one of the pieces of paper and read the word on it. Then tell the group one way that you can live like Jesus. You can then fold the piece of paper and put it back in the basket.

- **Say**: We're going to stand in a circle and pray together. We can pray with our eyes open. I'm going to say a phrase, and after each phrase you'll respond by saying, "Thank you, Jesus, for coming down to earth."
  o Jesus came down to earth to show us how to love.
  o Jesus came down to earth to show us how to be humble.
  o Jesus came down to earth to show us how to serve.
  o Jesus came down to earth to show us how to be grateful.

- **Say**: And all God's people said: (together) Amen. Let it be so!

Down to Earth: Children's Leader Guide

Older Children

- **Say**: This is our last week. We have learned why Jesus came down to earth.
- **Ask**: Why did Jesus come down to earth? What are some ways that you have loved others? What are some ways that you have been humble? What are some ways that you have served others? What have you been grateful for?
- Encourage children to share their answers.
- Divide the children into four groups.
- Have each group draw a piece of paper from the basket.
- **Say**: Read your piece of paper and, as a group, create a cheer to remind us why Jesus came down to earth.
- Encourage the children and help as needed as they plan their cheer. Allow enough time for all the groups to make a plan.
- **Say**: Come back together. We can pray with our eyes open. We are going to share our cheers as our closing prayer. After each cheer, we will respond, "Thank you, Jesus, for coming down to earth."
- Invite each group to share their cheer and the entire group to pray the response. Share all the cheers and responses.
- **Say**: And all God's people said: (together) Amen. Let it be so!

Prepare

✓ Before class, cut a sheet of paper into fourths. In large, bold letters, write *Love* on one piece of paper; *Be Humble* on another piece; *Serve* on another piece; and *Be Grateful* on the last piece. Fold the pieces of paper and place them in a basket.

✓ *Optional*: Prepare to record a video of each group's cheer, or take a group picture to send to the children for Christmas. It is also a good time to thank them for being in your class.

Be Grateful

Reproducible 4a

Grateful T-Shirt

Design your own T-Shirt. Think about how you can tell others to be grateful. Use different colors, shapes, pictures, and words to create a slogan or a design for your T-shirt reminding others to be grateful.

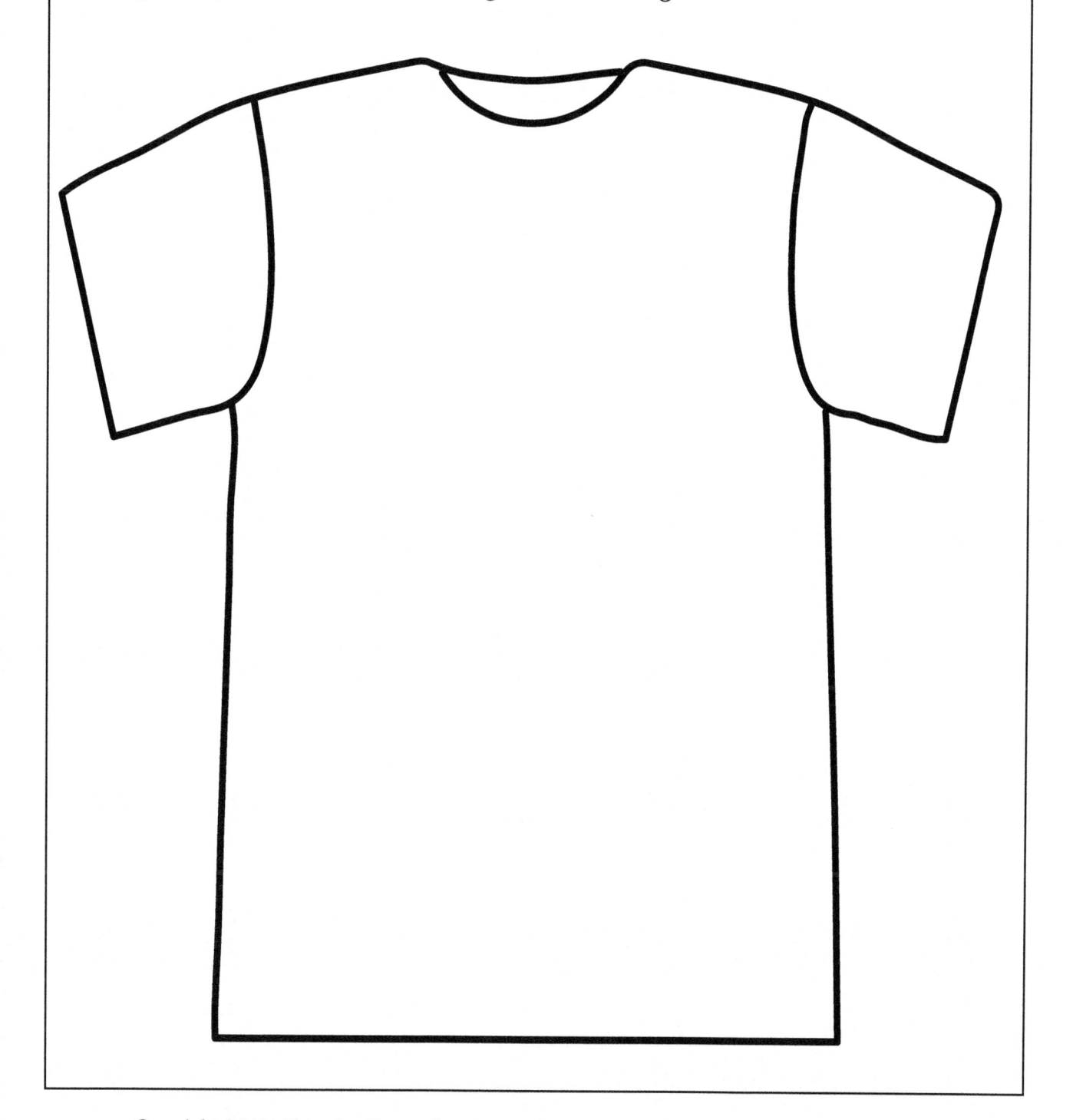

Reproducible 4b

Say Yes, Mary!
Based on Luke 1:26-56

An angel came to Mary and told her she was going to have a baby. The baby would be named Jesus. This baby would be God's Son!

Say yes, Mary!

Mary said, "How can this be?"

Say yes, Mary!

Mary went to visit her cousin, Elizabeth. Elizabeth told her, "God has blessed you, Mary! God has blessed your son, Jesus!"

Say yes, Mary!

Mary thought, "I will praise God! I will be grateful! I will be thankful!"

Say yes, Mary!

Mary sang a song: "God is Holy! God has done great things! God has chosen me to be Jesus' mother!"

Say yes, Mary!

Mary told everyone why she was so thankful. Jesus would come down to earth to show us how to love all people! He would show us how to be humble! He would show us how to serve others! He would show us how to be grateful!

Say yes, Mary!

So that's just what she did. Mary said yes!

Copyright © 2016 Abingdon Press • *Permission is granted to photocopy this page for local church use only.*